SOULSKIN

SOULSKIN

Marilyn Krysl

NLN Press · New York
Pub. No. 14-6754

The following poems have appeared in these magazines: "Soulskin," in *Another Chicago Magazine;* "The Blessing" in *Chicago Review;* "Transformations: The Terrace" in *Kansas Quarterly;* "Earth Sky Mandala" in *Notre Dame Review;* "Joint Venture," "Sustainable Development," and "Profit" in *Prairie Schooner;* and "Consumer, Sunset" and "Hymn to Hard Work" in *Spoon River Poetry Review.*

Copyright © 1996
National League for Nursing Press
350 Hudson Street, New York, NY 10014

The views expressed in this book reflect those of the author and do not necessarily reflect the official views of the National League for Nursing.

Library of Congress Cataloging-in-Publication Data

Krysl, Marilyn, 1942–
      Soulskin / Marilyn Krysl.
            p.   cm.
      Poems.
      ISBN 0-88737-675-4
      1. Healing—Poetry. 2. Nursing—Poetry. I. Title.
PS3561.R88S68   1996
811'.54—dc20   96-3149
                                                                      CIP

This book was set in Bembo by Eastern Composition, Inc., Binghamton, New York. The editor and designer was Nancy Jeffries. Cover design by Riva Sweetrocket. The printer was BookCrafters, Inc., of Chelsea, Michigan.

Printed in the United States of America

Contents

Acknowledgments

This work was partially funded by grants from the University of Colorado and the Colorado Council on the Arts.

I wish to express my gratefulness to the alternative healers whose work inspired me, and to the many generous health care workers in Göteborg, Sweden who assisted me in researching caring practices in that country.

I also want to thank Dr. Jean Watson who introduced me to those in charge of the Cancer Care Unit at Boulder Community Hospital where I was subsequently invited to research cancer care on the unit.

And I especially want to thank Dr. Watson in her capacity as Director of the Center for Human Caring. The Center explores new ways of advancing the art and science of human caring, ethics and clinical practice in nursing and the health sciences by drawing upon connections between these fields and the humanities, thus expanding the relationship between human caring, mind/body/spirit medicine, health and healing.

Both the Center and Dr. Watson supported me richly in spirit as I went about the work of researching and writing.

I am also grateful to my daughters, Hillary, Kristen, and Riva, and my grandchildren Kyle, Aaron and Hope.

Introduction

As we transit from the 20th century into the next millennium, the world is seeking a new direction—based not on laws of detached machinery and technology and industry, but a new order that is based upon laws of nature, natural order and natural processes of harmony and balance. Such an order resides not in a maldistribution of material wealth and health and power between first worlds and third worlds and all that comes between. The order being sought is for another knowing that rests on ancient, indigenous beliefs and practices of wisdom and traditions associated with knowledge of natural processes; such wisdom and practices are those known by Mother Nature and winds, seasons, and the sun and moon and animals that still roam where there is still land left to roam. These are the ways that are being pursued by the world today that may serve as an archetypal guide to order our meaning and existence. These are the practices we seek in spite of ourselves to keep ourselves sane and whole; these are the practices and inner knowing secrets that help us keep our connection with each other, other living things and the planet earth itself. Part of this new direction the world seeks today is based upon basic truths of human existence and our innate abilities to reach out and care for self and other and Mother Earth herself, if any of us are to be healed and survive.

After Marilyn Krysl's first venture into the inner life of human caring through the world of nurses and patients—a world she entered from that secure place as a prize-winning poet in the world of academe—she engaged in life-changing experiences that parallel what many seek today; that is, a new meaning about human existence and natural processes of life and death and how we can be in harmony in the midst of a universe that is out of natural order. Her venture into this search for a new direction affected both her own life and those who have read her poignant and powerful works, after a year as poet/writer in residence in 1987–1988 at the University of Colorado Center for Human Caring.

When she stepped lightly into her first nurse-patient encounters she felt and captured first hand the lived moments of pain, anguish, poverty, oppression, suffering, and existential despair that is part of the world of caring and healing that nurses and other health professionals encounter everyday, often without seeing. Nevertheless she witnessed and captured moments that are part of the world we all seek at some level to re-harmonize and re-member the natural processes of living and being and dying.

As Marilyn said to me after her first venture with us in the Center project, "My life has never been the same"; she conveyed that she felt she could not return to what was and who she was before that year's experience.

That intense world of caring and healing which she experienced then, in the '80s, was reflected back upon itself and to us in her now well known *Midwife and Other Poems on Caring* (1989, NY: NLN Press).

Now in this work, in the late '90s we see more clearly how her life has truly changed. We see first hand how she stepped off the page so to speak, from the life of the academic poet/writer to the other side of human existence where caring and healing were calling forth new responses. Marilyn Krysl has responded to this call to care and in this collected work we too are caught up in her life-changing world which plumbs the corridors and lifeways of the dying and destitute in Calcutta to the momentous marvels of nature, natural processes and moments that transform the living and dying.

Soulskin takes us into a deeper, more courageous and remarkable journey than *Midwife*, because in this work, Krysl is not just seeking a new adventure for gaining novel experiences for her writing, but is challenging her own being by pursuing authentic, humbling experiences of those who are striving to both live and die, to heal and be healed. Further, this writing attests to the human ability to serve others and life itself with dignity, humility and grace, when one is often confronted with only disgrace, humiliation, and neglect.

This latest work gives voice to those who have no voice to speak, no power to exercise, often no health nor basic sustenance, nor even sight to see, to realize, to acclaim their own being. Marilyn Krysl helps us to live the other side, even as we find it tears our soul and stirs our discomfort, often to an intolerable level, it also and ultimately inspires and uplifts the human spirit.

She literally gets inside our soulskin and touches the deepest dimensions of our humanity and inhumanity and in small, simple acts of caring helps us to re-discover why we care and why we must care, even when there is no acclaim nor reward. Perhaps it is soul care that we receive when we allow ourselves to respond to the call to care; perhaps if enough humans could be transported by Marilyn Krysl's soul-stirring moments we could recover and re-member our own cherished moments of connecting and serving another in their most vulnerable, darkest moments of need. That in itself is enough and must be enough if any of us are to sustain caring and humanity in the midst of this imperfect world.

If any of us are to face ourselves and our future with hope for a new order of possibility—if any of us are to go beyond not accepting what is, we too, can be called to care through this powerful work that helps us imagine what might be. It is through the most humane of human acts of kindness, concern, love, and service in the life of others most needy—recognizing ultimately that they are us, and we are them—that there is an "I that is we," that one person's level of humanity reflects back on all of humanity, attesting to Hegel's deep notion, that when one person is not free, no one is free.

In summary, Marilyn Krysl's work *Soulskin* offers up a sweeping landscape for healing and for transforming ourselves through our own inner and outer world where we witness and experience our own psychic flow that claims our being. She opens up a journey into our unknown recesses of human existence, away from the blare and tear of toxins toward a soft light of reflection and immersion into soul space that sustains and transforms and finally serves to both reveal and heal.

So here we travel with her on her journey of repose and courage, from Calcutta and Mother Teresa, to Water Lilies to Inner Sanctuaries, to Curanderas, to Incantations of Touch and Sound Healings, to Swedish Light, from Manifestos, Juntas, and Fights to Life and Lightness of Being; and finally to the United Nations.

The first becomes the last and the last becomes the first when "Hygeia Addresses the United Nations." In this closing/opening work, we are washed over, for in this poem, as the feet of an old woman are washed in Calcutta we are then moved to tears here in the United States and in the United Nations. The haunting personal refrain asks each of us about the politics of caring:

"tell me,
while I've been on my knees
washing the feet of old women
tell me—what have you done?"

Soulskin transports, transforms, informs and heals. It is part of the solution the world is seeking through its quest for a new direction—a direction based upon the laws of nature and the natural order of the simple—within the natural order, the simple becomes profound, the small becomes immense, the great encircles back on itself so that the smallest and most simple human acts restore and preserve our sanity, our dignity, our grace, our humanity, our humility, and ultimately through this natural order we heal our inner and outer universe.

Jean Watson, PhD, RN, FAAN
University of Colorado Center for Human Caring
University of Colorado Health Sciences Center
School of Nursing
Denver, Colorado

Preface

Over and over the world heals us.

Sometimes another person seems to be the agent. Sometimes it feels as though we heal ourselves. Sometimes we feel ourselves heal when we didn't know we were ill. Sometimes a particular place has a healing effect, or a piece of music acts like healing balm, or we are healed by paying attention to a sunset, or by being present at dawn.

Animals, birds and insects have healed me. Wind and grasses have made me whole again. I know I can count on the ocean. If I sit beside it long enough, I will be well. If I swim, I will be washed clean.

Over and over, observing my own healing, working with healers, I learn again that it is the world we're a part of that renews us. We become ill when we deny, in one way or another, that primal connection.

This book records many moments of healing in widely varying circumstances.

I offer these moments so that you may be aware and find your own.

Spring

I have loved
so many in this world

so long
that now this love

flows in me
like water

rising
from the core

of the earth,
pouring out,

where I am,
myself

the spring

I
SELF HEALER

We are engaged in transforming ourselves moment by moment, sometimes consciously and deliberately, sometimes intuitively. The shapes and sizes of these transformations are many and various. They happen when we have given ourselves completely—with our bodies, with our very beings—to our own healing, to another person, or to some thing alive in the world.

In writing *Soulskin* I became fascinated by the change that takes place when we move psychically from "dryness" to "wetness," from the glare of high tech, amoral, alienating, public space to private, wild, erotic space. There are myths and tales which address the loss of physical suppleness that comes with age and also the loss of psychic flow, flexibility and spontaneity that results when we solidify and become set in predictable patterns. I had read and been much moved by Dr. Clarissa Pinkola Estés' book, *Women Who Run With The Wolves,* and especially by her story that she named "Sealskin, Soulskin." The word "soulskin," was coined by her both in her story and in her poem, "Woman Who Lives Under the Lake," © 1980, C.P. Estés, *Rowing Songs for the Night Sea Journey— Contemporary Chants.** To fully claim our own presentness, we sometimes have to leave the surface spaces of our lives and go into psychic darkness. Such journeys are richly exhilarating. They open spacious landscapes which we have kept hidden from ourselves and the world.

Before I began the poem, I felt trapped and solidified in an urban landscape. It had become my psychic landscape, made of glass and metal and artificial light. And it was toxic. When it began to break up and my energy began to move, I felt I needed a very large, sweeping canvas in order to convey the sheer scope of this journey and the wild, transforming energy I was moving through.

*The term "soulskin" is used by permission of author C. P. Estés and Ballantine Books, a division of Random House, Inc.

Soulskin

I'm going away
from the blare and roar of these lites,
from electric florescent neon videolite,
from mercury vapor laser cameo bite lite,
from appetite lite, from grabbing and getting lite,
from sex lite, force lite, the Triumph of the Will lite,
from the Svenska helmet ceramic-plated flak jacket lite,
from the guerrillas and the government forces lite,
missile and the anti-missile and the anti-anti-missile lite,
away, away, away, away, away

from the lite of smiling while inside you feel sick
because you slit a throat before you went to bed last night
from the lite of smiling while inside you feel sick
because you said *Yes, I'll be empty so they'll give me the money*

from superselective electronic security system lite,
from Savings and Loan IMF deficit lite,
from the millions of parking slots empty at midnight lite,
from concrete and asphalt and headlight lite,
all night streetlight and graveyard shift lite,
from police lite, state trooper highway murder lite,
from beat up a woman run down a girl with a pickup lite,
from *I followed one of my impulses* lite

beyond which is the lite of young men
educated for steak, illusion and boredom,
and the lite of our failure to help them imagine compassion,
of our failure even to allow them to fail

beyond which is the lite of young women
educated for dietlite and small dreams
made pregnant and made to keep the baby,
made pregnant and made to give the baby

away: I'm going away
         from these lites, back to where

    it's dark, and there are
    smells,
            the smell of my lover
            on my body, the smell of
            good food, which, when I
            eat it, changes the smell
            of my body—garlic
            oregano cardamon heat sweat,
            my girl smell, my woman
            plankton smell, my
            organism smell

    and further back
            where I'm intelligent
            and whole, both liquid
            and a firmament, dream
            and hairy reality,

                        back through dolphin to plankton
                            to krill, and further back
                                into deeper

    dark
    where bird, snake, wolf
    drink at the edge of water
    where I too kneel, drink,
    see my face, smell my own
    smell, feel my own
    skin—oh my skin, sweet, supple, where did I

        drop it, leave it, lend it for a
            minute, my lovely leotard
            skin, my leopard skin, my

6

boa skin, my shimmering
   sex skin, my saffron monk's robe
   skin, my wet suit walrus skin,
   my SINGING AT THE TOP OF MY LUNGS skin
   and the skin of my tears, my grief

my grief for earth air fire water
   my tiny twittering
   birdskin, my great gallumphing
   mammoth skin, and my second skin
   for emergencies, my
       wet skin of vows, damp skin of prayers,
       of repeating the mantra and going
       slowly, don't hurry, speed
       kills, rush is
       aggression, go
       liquid,

       that's why I'm going

back, back into
   the dark, into the water, into the dark
     warm water, into the ocean, fathom
       by fathom, and further down, under
        the bottom
         where, in the dark,
          something is
            glimmering,
            glimpse of glistening

            membrane, a simmering
          shimmer, a liquid shawl
       of sequins, my slick, dripping
     sealskin, my
   oilskin, my rain soaked
soilskin, my

soulskin,
which, when I slide it
over my shoulders,
is wet and slick and sleek
and fitting, and

shines

as only the body can shine

with the light of the body, the soul

II

SELF AND NATURE

Nature is who we are. We are animals: we live in bodies and in these bodies roam the earth. I wanted to "re-member" the unspoken knowledge that we have when we live fully in our animal bodies and to suggest how profoundly this body knowledge enlivens the psyche, how often it sparks healing transformation, and how much it gives us of pleasure and deep satisfaction.

Transformation: The Terrace

Days of rain, and my soul without
      light. Leaden. I toss down the mat
         in the sun, strip,
            lie on my belly. Bells,

a carillon, noon, and I'm
      sweetly loose—all these linkages
         have more play in them
            than usual. Sheen of sun

everywhere on me, and I think of
      the museum, Lindstrom's
         Juliana, larger than life size,
            whiter, more naked: me,

free of any stricture but breath, stroked
      by the golden hand. Weeds
         between the paving stones, fluttering,
            a breeze riffling across me,

nakedness a sweet
      iniquity, my psyche a revelry,
         pure, pristine, and I'm
            a baby again, damp, dewy,

softened by the long bath before
      birth—without appointments, assumptions
         or possessions—richly endowed,
            newly arrived in this world.

Planetary

Notice how the foot,
    bare, fits the surface
        of the earth. How the arch
            lifts where the ground

rises a little. How only
    when you stand, feet bare
        on the ground, do you feel the grains
        of powdered dirt

are alive. Now you walk,
    each step in the print
        of one of those early others
            who first walked here

and chose this direction,
    and saw, against darkening sky,
        an orb, went toward
        firelight

and found food. Beneath
    this grass, the crust's
        hard gneiss,
            and beneath that

marble, its churning
    crystals, spinning, a glass animal
        rolling over
            as the earth turns,

and further down,
    at the core: liquid iron,
        boiling nickel. Feel
            with your feet: mineral energy

rises through diamonds,
      coal, the compress of petals,
            leaves, to meet you,
                  enters your body,

climbs the spiral
      staircase of the spine,
            the gene, greets blood,
                  floods the nerves:

you discover
      you are heat
            risen from the center
                of the earth.

Water Lilies

All morning, in this mild sun, forkful
by forkful, I heave off these quilts
of dry needles: dead fire.
Now the lids of the tanks
lie exposed, funerary, slabs
of ash, the lilies'

long urns. I open the first
lid: grayed skin, laid across
water. Tear it
with both hands, reach to the chalky
bottom. This is the place
they told us about, this is the place
where they lay

the dead gods. I have come to get down and
dirty with the ancients, to let the
juices in me loosen,
sweeten, to get my hands in the everlasting
ooze. Please,
let me be like these bulbs
fed by fire. Bleached
by darkness, soothed through winter
by the sway of water,
they have begun
to split and swell, row
upon row, layer on layer, the many breasts
of the Venus of Willendorf

filling. Now a rill, fiery,
runs through me. Something in me begins
to bow. I peel away
this blouse, damp
from my effort, slough off the dead
skin of routine, and now a tiny

rip, a tear, and there
at the hard core
of the heart

something snakes upward
and out: I
splay apart, the clenched self
flaring, I have become this wave,
the light
flowing all at once into the burning

moment. What glory
to come all the way open, an O,
generous
and obscene, green, airy as spray
of churned sea, fecund
as this silt the lilies lie in,
loosed, like them, to be
fully myself,

as in tank after tank
down the length of the greenhouse,
from each kernel, thin threads
like tiny vipers
begin their snaky
climb, each lengthening stem
becomes a floating
line, thrown up through
water,
where later, in shimmering air, on the pond's
lit surface,
these fiery tongues
bold blossom after blossom
will unfold

what cannot be held back:
pure glorious godhead,
their shimmering
a *now* moving on through time,
perishable, but risen
as only the sublime can rise
from bottom slime.

Earth Sky Mandala

The way wind
fits the grass it blows across

my body
fits this earth. I lay my length

across its curve. This grass
contains the sweetness

of the last rain, and below
the odor of

humus—stems leaves blossoms
transforming themselves

all the way down to where
the Cretaceous

keeps the imprint of the first
flowers. I won't want

to leave this life, but since
I must,

I can't think of a better place
to go. Imagine

becoming simple
as soil. I'll run at the same speed

as the turning earth.
Right now I'm half way

between those frilly fossils
and the stars.

Consumer, Sunset

All day I'm greedy
I think and think
what I want, I don't
stop wanting

Evening, and the sky
is many colors
These colors
have no names

They are not
manmade
We did not
produce this

Suddenly I notice
there is nothing I want,
nothing
I need

III

ALL MY RELATIONS

*Relations among us also spark transformations that
quicken our aliveness.* Hymn To Hard Work *came about
as I meditated the pleasure of strenuous physical work and
as I began to realize how much my pleasure in work had
been an inheritance from my mother. At first I thought of
the poem as praising her, but as the writing progressed, I
began to understand that the poem centered on the bond
between us, bound as we were by a common experience of
hard work and by a similar attitude toward it, an attitude
she surely handed on to me.*

Hymn To Hard Work

After a day of hard work I think back
to you, Mother, when I was a child,
as you stepped sweet smelling from the bath,
rosy with the heat of the water

and drowsy. I hear the bubbles' airy bursts,
the bath water goes, you wrap yourself in a towel,
a day's weight sunk to the soles of your feet,
this flesh the only wealth

you were sure of. From you I learned
to take full measure of exhaustion
and drink it down, make it mine. Tonight,
after a long, sweet day in the garden,

lifting forkful by forkful all this winter's
compost, I'm a wealthy woman. Every cell
is sated, there's money in my bones.
I'm my own filthy rich heiress

as you were, I've earned it as you did,
and as I rise from the bath, I honor you
as you were then, steamy, weary, filled
to the brim. Two women, burnished by labor,

polished to a high sheen like stones
in the ocean, by water and time and light
and air. Another day in the universe
belongs to us. As does this tiredness, this

gown, cloth of gold all the way to the floor,
which we shrug off, we let the whole thing fall,
and it feels good. Good to have stood beside you,
Mother, and worked beside you, good and hard.

It is in nature and in the world with others that we are erotic. The tactile is erotic, and so is shape. A water jar feels especially feminine, and any body of water, with its surface and depths and its ceaseless movement, suggests the psyche. On the bus in an Asian culture I felt my foreignness, and I could not speak the native language. Holding the jar was a way of being in live relation with the woman who owned it and she with me.

Bus: Women With Water Jar

The jar was red clay,
big around
as two arms, an earth
she would fill

with water. I took it
on my lap, held it
by the lip, leaned
around it. Let it

fill me. I, who had been
empty limbs and straight
lines, became then
so many fishes and loaves

that I could afford
to be generous again
and leafy green. Thus
she fed the multitude

that was me. Then came
her stop. I,
who had gained,
gave the jar back

full. And when she got off
I was happy
some of that red clay
had rubbed off on me.

All of us who must work indoors sometimes feel ourselves in an enforced alienation from nature. One day, attending a meeting of my department, I experienced acutely the uneasiness that often comes when I know much time will pass before I can go outside. My body seemed to shrink and close down to a minimum level of functioning. I scanned for something—anything—that would reconnect me, in whatever way, to the live world. A very small thing—the scent of soap in a man's shirt—served. It quickly gave me back a sense of my erotic self, and with the security of knowing who I was came the courage to get up and leave the meeting.

Erotic

The meeting is boring, and there are
no windows. We don't laugh, we don't
long. No drums, no rattles. No song.
This is not the way into the next world.

Then you come in, sit down beside me:
I smell the soap in your clean shirt,
imagine the hair all over your body,
and suddenly I'm warm blooded again,

species, genus, phylum, kingdom:
I nurse my young, I sing. I have
plans. I sweep out of the meeting,
stroll into green morning. Sun

noses my skin. How alive the animal
air is, and there's a place inside me
like grass the day after a soaking.
Yes, I accept the bouquet of fire.

On the street I sometimes feel alone, separated from the strangers I pass. Any bit of connection with a passing stranger can be a way to reconnect with myself and climb consciously back into the community of the live world. One day, in a strange city, I left my hotel to take a walk and met a man who had lost an arm. Sometimes those who have lost a part of themselves are given a gift. This man had been given a rare ability to be intimate which he had lacked before his wounding. Simply to be in his presence for a short time was healing.

The Blessing

It means a god has looked down
and seen you. I walk, talking

to the man with the pink plastic
arm. Where his hand should be

a hook, which he raises like a hand.
As he talks I understand what I want,

and now he tells me something
so private I cannot repeat it.

I answer, gesturing the way
we sometimes do when we are

talking. The way we sometimes do,
he lays his hook a moment on my hand.

I feel his fingers. In front of us
the street has become a brightness.

The culture of the West is geared to efficiency. Speed is a virtue. I like older people, those who are living at a slower, more gentle speed. In Göteborg there were several homes for the elderly that were especially thoughtfully geared to the lives of elders. With them one day while they were eating, I experienced a moment of heightened awareness in which I felt us all one weave, that weave illuminated by afternoon light streaming through a window. It was a momentary coming together of people and light.

Göteborg: The Old

There is moving food to and fro
on the plate, trying to get a bite
on the fork. Salad slides. Soup
refuses to ease itself

onto the spoon. And when you get
egg on your face, a woman beside you
says, "Henry, wipe your mouth." Naturally
your napkin has gone where such things go—

Friends, doesn't this prove
that those of us who wait would be wise
to notice how the same light
falls on the ones eating, the ones waiting.

I wrote Cancer Floor *while a friend of mine was struggling with cancer. This friend was a man, but in order to truly empathize, I needed to experience his pain in imagination as though it were my own. I tried to dissolve my boundaries, and more and more I did not feel separate from him. When my friend lost his hair, I remembered how much personal power women especially attribute to hair, and the poem became a meditation on that power in which my imagined history and my imagined present engage in emotional and transforming dialectic.*

Cancer Floor

In high school we had something
called standards. You couldn't wear
the same clothes two days
in a row, and on Thursdays

no green. Our gods were cruel
and made of chrome, like the hood
ornaments on the boys' Pontiacs,
and they demanded tribute:

so many bags of gems, so many
slaughtered lambs. We accused
the girl for the standard
reasons: her blouse, her breath,

her teeth. Her parents, who didn't
have a lot of money. Her hair,
which we wanted for ourselves.
I was the one who brought

the scissors. Beneath our cashmere
sweaters, we wore a glittering,
hard mail, and we told her
this was for her benefit,

so she could look like us.
I remember the feel of her hair,
handfuls of sapphires, spilling
from my fingers. Afterward

she was like a boat, set adrift.
Now, on the waters surrounding
this boat, many pairs of scissors
float toward me. Five of us

on the floor have lost our hair,
all of it, in handfuls. We told
ourselves that girl was the weak one,
the scared one. We told ourselves

we were calling the shots. Now
I know who really calls them,
and who the warriors really
are: the ones sent into battle

without armor, who live the last day
like any other.

IV

HEALERS

The curandera's art is almost always passed down through family lines. She senses which of her daughters or more often granddaughters is destined to become her successor. The text for this body of knowledge is the curandera herself. Her knowledge and wisdom are passed on orally and by example to her acolyte.

Diana Valasquez, the curandera with whom I spent time, stressed that it is important to see the individual as an inextricable part of the community, and to perform a healing which includes that community in some way.

Curandera

for Diana Velasquez

Bright spring day, and this young man
comes to me, black leather
jacket over shoulder,
hip style, but the feel
is of bile, held back: for him
nothing is moving, his body
has the density
of lead,
and he doesn't even notice, beside
the steps, my sizzling zinnias!
Gafas over his eyes, and on his bicep
tattoo of snake, tattoo of big breasted
woman. *Muy macho,*

but none of this junk
is any good. I say "Take off
those *gafas.*" Watch his eyes,
holes, where misery
prowls. Finally I say it: *You want
to die.* This is not an idea
new to this guy,
but catholics
are not supposed to give the finger
to God's creation.
"Come back in a week," I say,
"wear a black suit, bring me twenty-five
dollars. *Veintecinco,* don't

forget." I hire a coffin
any catholic would be
proud of. Lilies, the works. That day
comes, he comes, I point to the
coffin,
say, "get in
and lay down." He's so miserable

he does what I tell him. He
lays down, he's

muerto. Those who know him
come, the priest does his thing,
incense, we sing, ave maria,
we pray—then the viewing
of the body. One by one
we file by. I touch
his hand, he's

frio. Now people
tell his stories, how he was always
going away, would come if invited
but wouldn't stay, and his
daddy—I had to pay that man
to come—the *veintecinco*
went to him—
his daddy says his son was a real
redrojo, sick, and a weak
little starvling, wouldn't
suck enough
to keep a rat
alive. His daddy spits
when he says this. (As you can
imagine, married to such a man, his mama
has already

kicked the bucket.) Then the others
say it too—weak, sick, no good
as a friend, no good for a husband,
bueno pa nada, and sure not
happy,
so it's sad, very sad,
but he's better off

dead. They weep, they wail, they
go. I'm alone with this
muerto. And now
tears, like you wouldn't believe
that much water and salt
in one man. And he speaks: *I don't want to
die*. Sobbing
is medicine, it gets the blood
going, he's moving
now, getting warmer, all this
anguish
is energy, and I say
"Sit up. *Escucha*.
Your daddy didn't want you,
and your mama was too sick
to do you any
good." *Todavia,* he says,
I don't want to die. And I say

"Well of course not.
Now remember
those zinnias beside my door? Those zinnias
want you. And the grass too, *igualmente,*
the sky, the squirrels, stray dogs,
all underfed cats and mosquitoes,
Tweetie and his little
feathered friends—all the live world,
mi amigo, we want you." And he
looks at me for the first
time, climbs from the coffin,
and says *I'm cured!*
And I say

"You're not
done yet. I want you to water
those zinnias for me every day,
and you go to church, say some prayers
for the grass. And remember old Mrs.
Sanchez? Three mornings a week
she needs you—yes, you—
to walk her to the taxi, that's at 8:30
when she goes for her
treatment. *Y una cosa mas:*
you will visit
each person who came today
and take them a small
regalo, and when they say Here,
drink some coffee, do you want
sugar, you answer *yes,*

and you sit with them, and you
drink it, and you
look at them, and you
talk. Don't leave
until you talk to them!"

I made sure
he gave back
to the community. And of course,
after that,
he was well.

Remedios

Before I was born my grandmother
dreamed. She dreamed I would become
the curandera. When I was four
she began to teach me. When I was eight
she sent me to cure a little
boy. And when I was ten
I went for the first time
into the mountains to learn
the yerbas.

We are all of us poor:
pobreza of too much
pobreza of buying junk
pobreza of the cheaply made
pobreza of throwing things away
pobreza of hurry, hurry, rush rush
pobreza of noise, of restlessness
pobreza of politeness, of tameness
pobreza of not stopping to give thanks

When you turn away
When you push away
When you refuse
the presences around you—
     trees, grasses, water,
          the ground where you walk—

you will be sick

It is true that we are hungry
Know this
It is true that we own nothing
Know this
It is true that water knows when you enter it
Know this

Taste what you eat
Pay attention to the snake
Seek the presence of those who remember they are holy
Comfort animals
Listen to the wind
Honor your parents and your husband's parents
Do not steal, do not lie
Do not love a married man
Do not reveal your politics
Do not use your power for lotteries
Do not do anything that will hurt the community

Dandelion is for the heart
anil del muerto lungs and liver
And the good altimisa de la sierra
brings down the pressure of the blood

Drink snow melt
and when you dig roots, don't dig them all
Don't gather only for yourself
Gather for all the people

Shari Edwards, the sound healer to whom my poem is dedicated, had no predecessor from whom to garner knowledge. She has felt her way forward, intuitively educating herself, and her "text" has been her own experience. To the extent that her art required, she has educated herself in mathematics, chemistry and physics. Her own sensitivity to sounds others could not hear and the pain she witnessed in those around her motivated her to experiment and through long, painstaking work, to develop her art into a healing technique.

Sound Healer

for Shari Edwards

Everything
    is resonance. Each note of the scale
        resonates with the atomic number
            of one of the elements, with a color
                of the spectrum, and with the

placement of the planets around
    the sun. Your body has its
        note. If you're ill, this note can make you
            well. If in pain, this note
                diminishes that pain. Hum it,

the note that makes your whole face
    vibrate. Or ask your friend to play it
        on his flute. Now be still. There's a
            frequency
                each thing gives off—grass,

a balustrade, bare ground, a parked
    car. Things are what they are,
        and they are always
            sounding. Leaves do their clattering,
                soft maracas. Cushions

hush. Straight backed chairs
    din at a high, thin
        pitch. Where the hammock sags beneath
            the linden, its hum is golden.
                Applewood sounds sticky,

and the rhubarb's platters of leaves—
    a bitter twang. Light adds its
        overtones, sixths, sevenths. Plants
            in sunlight give off
                strands of sound, those in shade

fewer, the strands
    thinner. Even as one sound
        dies away, what surrounds it
            comes more clearly into hearing,
                and if you

listen, you hear the things of this
    world, and beyond, the background hum
        of the universe. *We know the sound*
            of the ecstatic flute. But we don't know
                *whose flute it is.**

*The quote is from Kabir.

Medicine Woman *is based on the utterance of the Navajo healer Flower That Speaks In A Pollen Way. I was startled by the beauty her words evoked, and by the power of this beauty. What I know about landscape became more and more emphatic: the beauty of the landscape constitutes power, a power we honor by careful preparation of our own appearance. We are a reflection of the landscape, reflected by the landscape. In the poem I felt compelled to emphasize beauty. I also had the instinct to write a poem that resembled a chant because there was a chant-like quality about the medicine woman's way of speaking. She taught by repetition.*

Medicine Woman

Yes, I accept the beauty of the world.
Necklace an arc of silver, turquoise.
Necklace an arc of silver, turquoise.
Yes, I accept the beauty of the world.

What is is. It cannot be seen.
You are sick when you refuse what is.
You are sick when you refuse what is.
What is is. It cannot be seen.

Bad not to have good shoes, warm clothes.
Lack of sleep makes you sick. Refusal of spirit power.
Refusal of spirit power. Lack of sleep makes you sick.
Bad not to have good shoes, warm clothes.

Don't just zero in on a schedule: be present.
Accept what is wild. This is the medicine.
This is the medicine. Accept what is wild.
Don't just zero in on a schedule: be present.

A shiny crust like locusts leave. A shell.
You see it on some people. This is poverty.
You see it on some people. This is poverty.
A shiny crust like locusts leave. A shell.

Sweet soap makes lather. Wash my hair for me.
I will wash your hair. The washing loosens me.
The washing loosens you. I will wash your hair.
Wash my hair for me. Sweet soap makes lather.

The trees were looking for you, and the mountains.
There were clouds, and sunlight, and there was night.
There were clouds, and sunlight, and there was night.
The trees were looking for you, and the mountains.

Wet hair shines. Sage, sand, stone.
A small bird flits past. The world is clean.
A small bird flits past. The world is clean.
Wet hair shines. Sage, sand, stone.

What is is. It cannot be seen.
What is is. It cannot be seen.
What is is. It cannot be seen.
Yes, I accept the wild beauty of the world.

Of those who work within our technologically "advanced" health care system many are alternative healers. They have become so through their own perseverance. I met Gail Pashleigh when she worked as a registered nurse on the Cancer Care Unit of Boulder Community Hospital. Her intelligence and sensitivity, strength of character and powerful presence seemed dimensions beyond the ordinary and suggested to me Innanna, the Sumerian version of the Goddess or Great Mother.

Innanna was a fertility deity, and Sumerians believed her mating with males filled the rivers, springs and wells, and thus ensured the flourishing of the community. Like other versions of the Goddess, she encompassed the four aspects: Good Mother, Terrible Mother, Muse and Witch/ Whore. Innanna's power was such that she was invoked as a protector when Sumer went to war. She could make you or break you. You wanted her on your side.

I honor in all these healers the rich mix of their knowledge of the natural world, their common sense, their courage, their imagination, and their grounded spirituality. They are women who recognize that we are woven inextricably to earth and that we cannot disregard this connection with impunity.

Innanna

for Gail Pashleigh

1.

What matters
is that light pour through me to the others

What matters
is that I feed the flame of being

What matters
is that they not prevent
the wind, the sand, the stars,
the body

What matters
is that they not prevent
earth, air, fire,
water

If they take away the great things
I will hold to the small things

If they take away the small things
I will hold to the immensity

I will stand in the way in my own wild body
I will stand in the way in my own wild body

I say no, and the door closes
I say yes and the door opens
And if the door closes against me
I stay until the door opens again

I know more than the others
I have gone further than the others
It is my work to honor
and to set the way of honor in you

Here, take this flame, this water, this food
Eat, drink, warm yourself   Live

2.

People need to say
        goodby to each other,
                certainly mother and daughter
                    do. Bring Elena,

I said, but her father
        shook his head—*She's only*
                seven, he said, and did what he
                    wanted, sent his daughter

shopping
        with her aunt. This was a man
                who locked doors, and not once
                    lingered, looking up

at stars, who had not embraced
        his own, ferocious
                life. Just before his wife died
                    he walked out of the room.

Elena's aunt
        brought her a few minutes
                later. When she
                    came, when she said

"Can I stand by the bed?"
        I said, "Honey, of course." I
                won't forget the look
                    of Elena's

spine, that fine stem,
>   hair in two braids,
>   pinned up like two hands,
>   praying. Later

I found the tablet paper,
>   folded three times,
>   laid next to her mother's
>   ear. I washed her mother's

body, the way I do,
>   making sure I touched her
>   everywhere, one last time.
>   Then I taped the little note

to her breastbone. I sent Elena's
>   cry, like a hound, bounding
>   down that tunnel—at the end of which
>   they say there's light—into the ground.

V
CALCUTTA

In the summer of 1994 I worked in Calcutta as a volunteer in the Kalighat Home for the Destitute and Dying administered by Mother Teresa's Sisters of Charity. The air was diesel, the traffic slow moving sludge, and every day more refugees poured into the city from Bangladesh. On the bus I'd stand—seats reserved for women were likely to be taken. Most of us were coughing, sneezing, feverish. Guards at the entrances to each hospital floor let pass only those who could prove they had an appointment. Sometimes those seeking entrance turned frantic, bringing on a small riot. Everywhere there was an air of the crucial. Each person kept an eye out for theirs. Civility wasn't particularly a virtue, but on the other hand one was spared the pretense of civility.

In this atmosphere of crowding and scarcity, the Sisters of Charity's establishment stood out in relief. The atmosphere in the hospice was one of simplicity. Partly this is the result of Mother Teresa's vow of poverty. She wishes in her life and work to honor the way the poor live necessarily. *Accoutrements* were stripped away. Daily routine centered on what was essential for body and spirit: meals, baths, the changing of linens, the *agape* of an embrace.

Death was a common, daily occurrence.

Love and affection were as common as rice, bananas.

An atmosphere of simplicity is deeply affecting. When we live at this essential level, *there is no shortage*. Set off from both scarcity and plenty, small happinesses took on size and substance. Kindness acquired immense value. Those I cared for gave care back to me, and patients looked after other patients in significant and touching ways.

Simplicity creates an atmosphere of beauty and repose. I left for work every day aroused and eager. Often I'd think of lines from Walt Whitman: *I am larger and better than I thought. I did not know there was so much good in me.* I remembered these lines not with a sense of self-satisfaction but rather to confirm that *simplicity makes a space in which we are able to recognize that we are abundantly endowed.*

While I came and went in this city where poverty is vivid, the rhetoric of market economics kept spontaneously occurring to me. Terms like *joint venture, devaluation* and *investment opportunity* seemed vastly ironic in this landscape. Thus these phrases have become titles for some of the following poems.

The city of Calcutta, plagued by overpopulation, poverty, and environmental degradation, is a place of anguish. The poem Calcutta *sets the scene for those that follow. It also alludes to a phenomenon which occurs with fair frequency now in the subcontinent, a phenomenon referred to as bride burning, which is eloquently articulated in Dina Mehta's play* Brides Are Not For Burning. *In the play a husband's family takes out an insurance policy on his new wife, then persecutes her so mercilessly that eventually she commits suicide by locking herself in the kitchen and setting her sari on fire.*

Calcutta

Hell is other people.
  —Jean Paul Sartre

Not Dante's hell, but Sartre's. At mass Mother
Teresa sits in back, another woman
praying for bread. In the street a woman passes:
her basket brims with blossoms. Goats nose garbage.
Crows dive for tomato skins, then scatter.
The rich get richer and the poor multiply, but die

more quickly, with less glory. Some will die
by accident, some by design. *My mother*
set herself afire. The heart eats ash. A scatter
of crows, and you can't hear the sea—that woman,
her ancient, muttering presence, mouthing garbage,
crashing her cymbals. Mother Teresa passes

the bread, the wine. Sirens. A Diesel passes
in the street, the air thick. Someone is dying
somewhere. A girl sifts this pile of garbage,
and the Golden Shower's petals fall at her mother's
feet. (Husband's family needs the woman's
dowry, please, for VCR.) Scatter

of shops. The river, in this light, a scatter
of coins slung across water. The river passes
the phosphate factory, turns black. A woman
finds a bit of bread, eats. She dies
next day, not far from where she ate. Mother
of God, you with death in your mouth—garbage,

cracked teeth—pray for us: this is the garbage
children pick through at night. And we are scattered
bits of soul. (Hands, reaching for Mother's
hem.) Even the coins are worn thin, passed
from hand to hand ten billion times. Dying
children don't cry: they watch your eyes. A woman

burns, lives to tell another woman.
Medicinal plants near the factory sicken. Garbage
floats like petals, bits of bread. You die
like incense spreading on the air. A scattering
of ash, a flute, the pyre disappearing. I pass
the ghat: a girl calls out, begging her mother

for something to eat. Her mother slaps her. I'm
a dying woman, passing by. Garbage
as dirge. Look: those scattered crows converge.

Devaluation

Somewhere in the past, someone
broke her wrist: the way you'd
break a foot to bind it. Hand
to chest, above left breast,

fingers splayed: flesh corsage.
But it was her right arm
that alarmed me, straight up
to take the money: fist tight,

and her eyes, swollen shut. Sealed
writ. When something's so wrong,
there's nothing to do but begin.
Come, blind, into the ceremony

of hands. Unwind, slowly, the torn
sari, now a little solo of soap,
water, tremolo of towel. Her moan
worn thin: I moan in return,

primal song we two now sing, for one
must not sing alone. This smoldering
om our horizon syllable, uttered
longing the rhythm we rock on:

so our singsong koan goes on—
and her fist stays shut as stone.
But who rocks whom? Come dawn,
I lay her down, go home, doze

with my clothes on. Wake amidst
the light's incense, sensing some
immense, minuscule shift. I go
as though from the first washing

into morning. In the sickroom
she in whose body I rocked is dead.
The other sick ones hungry. Naturally
we're out of bread, tea. Of some things

there can never be enough: shrouds
one thing we don't run out of. I,
who come from a rich, smart country,
work the girth of her fist loose:

pais, less than a penny's worth.

Joint Venture

Shanti can't speak—sweet, flowing
talk, as we know it, not an option.
How came she to be this wail—
she wants something, or does not

want something to happen. Forty
and handsome, a chiseled Lakshmi,
someone I might have fallen
in love with, in situations other than

this one (say swanky dorm, Amherst,
or Smith. Or U.N. delegation,
evidence on Genital Mutilation).
Now everything except food's an invasion.

I talk up the glories of obligatory
bath—"Mother Teresa says you have to"—
ply repertoire of international
motherese: *feel this nice water,*

nothing terrible will happen,
I won't let it—while lorries
galumph past, lumbering the daylights
out of any possibility of beauty,

and Shanti wails. Crows pick walk
through trash, scammers, unabashed,
work the street here in the diesel
diaspora, the day's sweat a caul

I don't want. Sister Luke sweats
with us, but we're without caudle
for the wailing woman, and I'm
coming down with something, feverish

(though who isn't), stomach queasy.
Now Luke throws up her hands, leaves us.
I start the gown, careful to be slow,
left hand through sleeve, over elbow,

maybe this wail's a mantram, Shanti
repeating Hail Marys the only way
she can. I hear it then, the darkened
rhythm rises, turns, swerves upward,

and higher, gliding, now speeding
to the place where the pneumonic wave
breaks, flows out, slides back, recedes
in ocean's turning churn, where,

slowly, it will build again: how
long in its coming, this eloquence
of our brute longing, to my ear—
sung to me here near noon, sun

climbing up through the body, by she
who can't speak or walk out—to me,
who can say what I want exactly
and stroll out, free, but lonely.

Healing

The beds are low, you have to
          kneel
before the altar of the one asking
          for water. Remember

when the train rocked you to sleep,
that thief
          put the money back. I hold
             the cup to Dadima's

          lip. Her fingers,
fine sand blown by wind. Her hand, my hand,
             here is the door of the hand
opening

into that stuttering
          art: healing: ancient, mute,
             long gone from my body, stolen
from my fingers, and for centuries

          blank, now come
back: moving in me now like my own
awareness, streaming through me,
             a cry: so that I

          lift her, body to body,
rocking on the fulcrum of the one
             universal syllable: the body's
horizon note

          is a moan, uttered over and over,
this, and our rocking
             needle and thread, binding together
giver and taker, I, and she also, taker

and giver, that looping
circle, under
                         and over: you cannot tell one
from another. We are

         the heat rising around us, the
drumheads of our skin,
and then, as though lacings of a bodice
break, go

         slack, blood rushes
back, and her skin and mine
                    ignite with the bloom of those million
gardens: each many faceted

moment fanning out from the moment
                    before. My breath, her breath,
         thieves, let go
alive. You have to be close

                    to the ground
         to hear the horses'
hoofbeats. You have to feel
the dirt with your hands

to know who you are. Now the thief
         slips away. My purse
                    bulges,
coins, bills, jewels spilling over, filling

my hands to spend, to give away. You, here,
         drink this water. Take this
money: I know nothing.
         I am just now learning.

Foreign Aid

There is fire in us, around which the gods
    hover, our burning theirs, theirs
        ours, or say we do each other's
            burning, our work in this life to be
                enflamed, in fiery communion

with the other, those above with those
    a little lower, those lower with the ones higher,
        so that in blazing beyond ourselves,
            the gods and we, their
                human forms, learn, in the stretch,

humilitas. Now watch: blind Aruna
    leans on my arm, sputtering in the language
        of the spheres. Thin, bent, octogenarian,
            under the press of urgency Aruna
                leads me down the aisle, into

the hall, up that step and into
    the stall, where, gods, goddesses, all of us
        squat. Excrement is the universal
            leveler. It brings the mighty down
                to earth. Though no one's required

to stay there, certainly not regal
    Aruna, who merely resembles her icons,
        subcontinent versions of Plato's
            perfect forms: Lakshmi, Menachshi,
                Mother Kali, or is it Persephone

or Aphrodite—even Venus has been known
    to splay like this beside some mortal
        more able than herself—one of us runs
            water in the bowl, places Aruna's hand
                on the rim: she feels the familiar

shape, dips in, washes herself, reaches
for my arm—Great Mother Aruna, doing
another mortal a favor—and step by inching
step, this fiery lady leads me back
to bed: we find the edge, she eases

herself down. One thing's not done:
little clay bowl, her spittoon. Blest
briefly with sight, I place it in her palm.
Hear her voice, fierce, up from the
guttural: the gods have done well

and so has she. As for me, I've learned
to follow the blind. I watch hot sparks,
those blazing bits of flame, rising
around the god: Aruna sits, and when
phlegm gets to be too much, spits.

Altar

I do it the way the Saraswati
wants it. She wants the bedpan
handy, I go get it. She wants
the capsule ground. I grind it,

mortar and pestle this pill to powder,
bring it to her with a glass of water.
Wants the fan turned off, I oblige,
a sheet, I unfold one over her thighs,

a biscuit, please, I slip her this sweet.
I'm the servant girl, running
and fetching, bringing and clearing
away. Saraswati throws herself

into the autocrat, ordering me first
this way, then that. Today her highness
taunts me. *Why you do it!* A hiss, a whisper.
You are slave! she cries. *Bring me bread!*

I steal a slice when the nun's
not looking. Take it to Saraswati.
Suddenly the aristocratic brahmin
sees: how weak those powerful were,

how strong she was. She slides out,
crouches, forehead to stone floor. Now
there is no more bread, no water,
no capsule, no fan, no biscuit,

no bedpan. No sheets but shrouds.
The master's voice has gone dumb,
the servant girl can't see.
Saraswati bows, though not to me.

Dead Weight

The speed of light
is running down

Now the many colors of Nirmila's skin
take up their cloaks
and go

Once an airy
place, filigree
through which the breath
blew back and forth,

Nirmala was mostly wind,
and water. Now the fires
of the goddess at the center
of the temple

have gone out. Now there is
earth. She whom I carried
each day to the bath
is more than I can lift.

This is what they mean
when they say *dead weight:*
our flesh, emptied, collapses,
every atom closes down.

White dwarf, dead star.
Before we become
dust, this
is what we are.

Kalighat

Day after day the city's dim, pressed
down. High heat but little light,
air redolent with soot, and our labor

low to the ground, bending over
the feverish with water, kneeling to feed
the weak with a spoon. But once in a blue

while, after dawn, the pall falls away
and there's sky. If you climb to the roof
then, and look down on the proliferation

of men with bundles, bags, women
with babies, a rack of bangles
selling briskly, the buyers and vendors

of bananas and Kali idols bartering
to beat the band, and kids, playing
tag, slipping past an array of ripe

mangoes, tearing off through loudspeaker
blare, muscling the air, where kites
sail the vault, that blue rising

like the lit climbing of cathedral
ceilings—you may feel this pulse
in your own blood is reason enough

to descend with rag and pail, and,
while sirens wail beyond the drone
of the call to prayer, kneel, scrub

the floor below the arched doorway.

Sustainable Development

. . . there shall not be left
one stone upon another
that shall not be thrown down.
                    —Luke 21:6

We're made of water, carbon, ash of dead stars.
Salwari waits. We wait with Salwari, live
her suspension—hold your breath, breathe, hold
your breath. Death, that friend, doesn't come. The crucible
turning slowly, but turning. Slowly, I turn
her body for her, when she asks me. Sister Luke,

caustic: "God has gone out." *In patience* (St. Luke)
possess your soul. Here you can't see stars
or trees. The fans don't work. You toss, turn,
burn. Fever, the body's white noise. You live
from meal to meal, if you can eat. The crucible
abrades those open wounds. I kneel, hold

still: cut away the dressing. Salwari holds
to what she can find. Doesn't flinch. St. Luke:
not a god of the dead but of the living. This crucible
the hour: swab, gauze, tape. That star
the sun moves on. They say that those who live
with pain make profit. Personally, I doubt it. I turn

again toward this requiem of bone. She turns
her head: In English: "I die soon." I hold
her hand. Kiss each finger. While we live
there is this body. *This is my body* (Luke
again) *broken for you*. I walk home. No stars:
the stars don't come out, not in this crucible

Calcutta is. From medieval Latin, *crucible:*
lamp beneath a crucifix. Her people turned
her out: her broken leg, not set (the stars
are listening) healed crippled. Salwari doesn't hold it
against her father, or the new wife. St. Luke:
you shall be betrayed by parents, brethren. Hers live

on rice they grow, when they can grow it. They live
on what they earn, theirs another crucible
turning, like hers, the sluice anguish. St Luke:
There shall not be left one stone on another. I turn
her hips, shoulders. She can't eat, can't hold
a cup. She wants to sleep but can't. The stars

are other suns. We live alone. The crucible
turns, stills. Luke sobs, holds herself.
We're made of water, carbon, ash of dead stars.

Profit

I stand Shanti up, take her weight to the toilet,
bring Shirmila a bedpan, lift her onto the bedpan,
find the bowl into which blind Aruna spits phlegm,
turn on Uma's fan, feed her rice with a spoon.

I wipe Saraswati, wash bedpan, bring it back,
now Bactrim for Hasina—but today we're out of Bactrim—
shift Praba onto her side the way she wants,
though it hurts her to move or to stay as she was.

Chitra complains—she wants curry but no rice.
Savitri hates wet. I change her, and the sheets.
Hema waits a long time for a dry sarong,
then I fail to knot it the way she likes it.

Our voices rise like the cries of mynas,
warning, praising, scolding, English, Bengali,
the broken winged ones and me with my pitcher,
its beak pouring hundreds of drinks of water.

Troublemakers all, myself included. Now I kneel,
bowl and spoon, choruses of mouths to be fed.
Topaz trouble, sapphire trouble, emerald trouble.
Diamond trouble. This trouble has become my bread.

Interpreter

for Divya Satia

Speak for me. Tell her
I'm going away. Tell her
I see the way she's lucky—
how she got as a baby those fine

bones, and food enough,
those first years, to make
those good bones big. A strong
skeleton's serviceable,

just as the little black sheath
is chic. Say I long to see
her frame fleshed out
with wealth. Say I imagine her

filthy rich, full of piss
and vinegar, and tell her
those clamoring eyes of hers,
like the first cries of birds

opening dawn, lift me
from dimness. Say I have
taken those cries inside me,
so when I sit alone and sing,

their clamoring calls me
out of singleness
into the ring of noon.
Say I imagine her finger's

tip following a line
of print, in a book I wrote
to say these things. Say
please she must learn to read,

for I believe the word
is another bodying forth
into the good, green world
where, without it,

we cannot fully meet.
And I would meet her here—
this is all there is—this
shifting light and air,

a wave on which things come,
then go—and now say this:
great are the forces arrayed
against our meeting. Though

I won't say it won't be so,
or may, this is my last
day. She has from me
the only word I gave:

my name. Now say that what
I lacked came back filled
full. Say, so she knows,
I go. I won't be back.

VI
SANCTUARY

If our healing is complete, we not only remember our connection with others and the biosphere: we find ways to live consciously within those connections. Our actions are shaped by the fact that we know our living impacts these other lives.

In thinking about this great sphere of which we humans are a minute part, I began to speculate about the concept of sanctuary. In history sanctuary has taken the form of finding safety from persecution in religious communities. There was a place you could go and be safe. In our own time Jim Corbett and his friends assisted refugees from El Salvador until this helping across national borders became a modern sanctuary movement in the United States. There was, for a while, a place Salvadoran political refugees could go and be safe.

There are other, less dramatic and less publicized instances of sanctuary in our time, not the least of which is the political asylum nations offer the citizens of other nations. But as I meditated on sanctuary, I began to see it not simply as a religious or political concept, but as a social, cultural, racial, economic and gender phenomenon. If we say, for instance, that there is such a thing as economic sanctuary, we are forced to note that some of us have much more of it than others. Nor can we ignore the fact that there is an economic sanctuary in the West which insulates us from the suffering of others—those in our own country who suffer material hardship and those who suffer it in other nations. For the majority of people in Asian, Indian, Middle Eastern and Latin American countries there is no economic "place" they can go and be "safe." This exposure to suffering is a profound fact of their lives.

It is also a profound fact that most of this suffering of exposure is experienced now by nature, and among humans, by women and their children. Political, social, cultural, economic and gender factors are intertwined, but wherever economic poverty is a fact, species and gender play a very large part in determining who will benefit from scarce resources.

We think of the word junta *as denoting the military brass who seize political power and take over a civil government. Often government by* junta *is corrupt government.* Manifesto *came about because I felt acutely the stress of living in a culture which is shaped by a junta mentality. It is a culture in which humans are perceived as set off and divided from the rest of the natural world.*

I had been in the library reading through lists of extinct species and endangered species. The vastness of this destruction was literally unimaginable—who can fully picture the detail of suffering on this scale? And yet it is a writer's function to imagine the lives of others, not just other humans but all others, including plankton, including water, soil, stones. Though I could not produce a canvas adequate to the subject, the knowledge of this huge suffering impinged. I wrote Manifesto *out of my need to declare allegiance to an undivided world.*

Manifesto

The gods who divided us
were no gods
but a junta
with an idle afternoon

Look in the mirror, they said
You're different
You're not like the ones
with fur, with feathers

Nor are you like the ones with leaves
or the ones who slide through water
You're not like those reptiles,
the ones with scales, and fangs

Don't mix things up
Don't confuse the issues
Some belong one place
Some in another

There have to be laws
Because you're special
we're sending you
to a special place

It's what god wants, they said
It's what's good for the country
Then they kissed us
and put on the blindfolds

But there are ways
to remember how it was
before they burned numbers
in the palms of our hands

Feel inside You're like the others
You're like the stones
You're like the water,
You're like wind, like fire

like the ones with roots and seeds
the ones with fins
The ones with mouths, eyes, skin
The ones with hearts, with wings

I wrote the section of Sanctuary *about the Swedish mother and the Kurdish women shortly after visiting Göteborg in 1990. The visit had nudged me to examine my own cultural assumptions about beauty and about religious iconography, especially the way in which we sometimes use images of beauty and religious images to romanticize and promote our cultural assumptions and to obscure damage caused by our way of life. I might have ended my poem there, for the suffering of Kurdish women certainly stands in contrast to the relatively easier lives of women in the West. But when I read the story of the Filipina maids, I perceived that their story too was part of the global matrix of economic sanctuary, and I wanted to include it in the poem. Obviously there are many, many more stories which fit this paradigm. I like to think that in the future my poem may continue to expand.*

Sanctuary

1.

Say a Hail Mary
for the Filipina girls,
good Catholics, who got down on their
knees, every day, in good faith, and
repeated, dutifully, their
Hail Marys—girls
whose families kissed them goodby (in good
faith), packed them (dutifully)
off to Kuwait, where, people said,
the Kuwaitis needed maids
and you could make a lot of money
very quickly. So

handy, these young women—and so
many! Good Catholic girls, who'd eventually
be married off anyway, and
besides, they were (dutifully)
handy, as girls are, and abroad
they could actually do something
useful, producing a handy cash flow
for the family back home, thus
(dutifully) bolstering
the local economy, and generally
beefing things up

back in Manila. Those girls
were practically
money itself, and so,
off they went (in good faith) to Kuwait, where,
it turned out, there was soon
a war on, which meant
soldiers—soldiers
who were winning, and soldiers

who weren't. Quite a difference, you'd think,
between winning and losing,
but according to the girls you could not tell
the difference. They were soldiers,
and they did the same

things—things soldiers
do, because they're
(dutifully) soldiers, far from
home (in good faith), and in war
the rule of law
doesn't apply, and anyway
they're afraid and bored
and homesick, and sick of
the ways of their mothers and fathers, who
brought them up (dutifully,
in good faith) to be
good boys, but not to let anyone
push them around, and

also they just wanted to have some
fun, because there was the chance
they might die, and you want
some fun
before that happens. And

there were those (handy)
Filipina girls,
right there, so many, so young, and so
pretty, oh yes (though it hasn't
been mentioned), very
pretty, AND
they were also (in good faith)
virgins, and you know

how volatile

a young, pretty virgin
can be, (dutifully) far from
home, and homesick, (in good faith)
in a foreign
country, where, temporarily,
the rule of law
doesn't apply.

And when, back home
in the Philippines, it
"became known"
what these soldiers (in good faith)
had done to the good, Filipina
Catholic girls (some of whom
had finally had it
with all those Hail Marys
to no avail, and
in good faith decided
it was their duty
to themselves
to go public)

a good, Catholic Filipino
senator, grinning dutifully on
camera, remarked in good faith
that those girls
should learn
to enjoy it. For the Filipina girls, there was

no sanctuary. Say
a Hail Mary
for them.

2.

This is sanctuary—Hail Mary—
this sunlit alcove where a woman

feeds her baby. Notice the gown
fallen from her shoulder, her skin

the muted cream Old Masters chose
to paint the Virgin,

as though God's mother
had been the wife of a burgher

from Minsk. But the ideal
is a snare: I must be

careful. I am as hungry as anyone
for beauty, and that light

through the open window
seems to clothe her, and to radiate

from her. Let me be
clear: this calm, this plenty,

this shower of gold across
maternity,

in this city, sleek with wealth
on the Swedish coast,

is sanctuary. (Think television,
those Kurdish women

walking the mud slick road, barefoot,
a baby bound to each back,

all they own balanced on their heads,
holding the youngest

by the hand, coaxing the older ones
to keep walking. Cut,

see them huddled at a flimsy
fire. Flecks of snow blow across

the screen, and the network
cuts to an ad for a fast car.) I

will not lie. I will not
call this Swedish mother

madonna. I will not say *like the bloom
on a pear*. I will not say *God,*

or the word *holy*. I will say only
this: another Swedish mother

feeds another Swedish baby,
while across the bay,

stevedores unload a freighter
of Chiquita bananas from Paraguay.

*On a flight from India back to the United States I
began to write* Hygeia Addresses the United Nations. *I
was moving through a very complex transformation,
traveling from the culture of India back to the West.
Moving from the East back to the West is always difficult
for me. I know I am going from a place where economic
poverty is a fact for many, many people to a place where
over consumption is the order of the day. From a place
where communal ties are honored and prized to a place
where selfishness is considered healthy and normal. From a
place where nature is revered as essential to a place where
technology dominates consciousness. From a place where the
pace of a day has a human scale to a place where efficiency
is the highest priority. From a place where spiritual practice
is a part of diurnal life to a place where the value of a
spiritual practice has little venue and where the very
existence of the spiritual dimension is in question.*

*I wrote the poem to try to ease the dis-ease I felt in the
midst of this transition.*

Hygeia Addresses The United Nations

Ladies and gentlemen, pick any continent
either north or south of the equator,
and presto: a road
cut through sand,
a trail across ice, a way
slashed through fronds,

and at the end of these
a stand of trees,
a clearing,
a hut, where, while the eldest girl
turns earth and tends the smaller children,

the woman who is her mother
walks six miles to gather wood, draw water

and now squats, bent over a pot,
stirring something.

The soles of her feet are the color of earth
cracked, like earth,
nails black as the earth
and horny.

We are ancient.
We have always been ancient.
This is our strength.
This is our weakness.

Both ways destroy us.
Both ways hold up the world.

Tell me, ladies and gentlemen,
you who cry up the armadas of the modern,
who bang the drum of the slum slung cities,
who clang the giant flag of state,

tell me,
while I've been on my knees
washing the feet of old women,
tell me—what have you done?

VII

DEATH, LIFE

It is a truism that the transformation of death is a healing out of suffering. It is also true that many of us, shaped by the culture of the West, still view death as something to be feared, rather than as a natural part of the earthly life cycle. It is a failing of our culture that fear of death has been so pervasive that it is now the custom in Christian nations that family members do not take care of the body of the dead person. To cut ourselves off from the newly dead makes our grieving more difficult. Surely this abandonment also causes grief to the beloved person.

I am drawn to the Buddhist practice of the family washing and dressing the body of the dead person and keeping it in the home for three days of mourning. It is also customary that after cremation or burial, family and friends read Buddhist prayers each day for forty-nine days, because they believe the dead can still hear and are struggling to find a good rebirth. Belief in reincarnation is surely reflection of the fact that death and birth are not separate and opposing events but part of an endless material and spiritual cycle.

Let us not separate what is whole.

The Dead and The Living

You who have loved me, listen to me now
I came into this world whole   Whole let me go

Do not deliver me
into the gloves and knives of strangers

Wash me yourselves, you my intimates
Use your hands, touch me everywhere one last time

Silt the openings into my body with fragrance
Light torches in each of the four directions

Place beside me my instruments
My crystal, my comb, the cup I drank from

Say how I lived, if well, if badly
Tell my story   Call me by name

On the fourth day lay my body in the ground
Let the good worms take me to the underworld

Or build a pyre of apple, oak, cherry
Let the flames of long burning consume me

Or bear my body to the heights, lay me on stone
Leave me to the high winds and the sun

Or lay my body in the bottom of a small boat
Then let this craft drift out

Give alms in my name for forty-nine days
For forty-nine days read me the prayers

On the last day say the last words the last time
Let me go into earth, into air, fire, water

Let me go into the pure gullet of the vulture
Love me and let me go, as I am bound

A contraction is a wave in the passionate transformation that is birth. In Swedish maternity hospitals there is the custom of the father helping the mother through a contraction in the way the following poem describes. As I watched a couple experience the woman's contractions together in this way, I was reminded of works by Michelangelo in which he captures lived moments of intense emotion in stone. I perceived this couple momentarily in one of those living moments sculpture enshrines. In their focused concentration, in the ardor of their attention, they seemed lifted as one whole to the light.

Contraction

She has locked her arms around
    his neck, and hangs, she
        and the child within her
a pear, weighing down

its bough, as he
    takes that weight, steadying her,
        his mouth at her ear,
whispering sounds like new

leaves, each whisper
    a version of *yes*. So the father
        enters birth: stepping
with the mother

into these moments, they become
    one figure, hewn from stone,
        pure energy—one flesh nerve bone—
for as long as the contraction

lasts. Then it's over—the sag
    of her sigh, then his. He
        lets go, her arms
fall away, they become, once more,

two people, without
    the advantage of marble,
        polished by the sweat
of what they've accomplished,

facing each other
    across the small,
        distinct distance
of the human.

About the Author

Marilyn Krysl is the author of five books of poetry and two books of short stories, as well as numerous essays, articles and reviews. Her work has appeared in *The Atlantic, The Nation, The New Republic* and many other journals, as well as in *O. Henry Prize Stories, Pushcart Prize Anthology* and the anthologies *Lovers, Vicious Circles* and *For A Living: The Poetry of Work.* "Mercy" won *Negative Capability*'s 1994 Award for Fiction, and "Jet Set Chronologist" won *Spoon River Poetry Review*'s 1995 Editor's Award for Poetry.

She has been the recipient of a grant from the National Endowment for the Arts, grants from the Colorado Council on the Arts, a residency at Yaddo and an Artist's Grant from *Earthwatch*. She is Director of the Creative Writing Program at University of Colorado, Boulder, has taught ESL in the Peoples' Republic of China, served as Artist in Residence at the University of Colorado School of Nursing's Center For Human Caring and performed at International Caring Conferences and at the annual conference of the National League for Nursing.

In 1992 she spent four months in Sri Lanka as a volunteer for Peace Brigade International (PBI) and in 1994 as a volunteer at the Kalighat Home for the Destitute and Dying administered by Mother Teresa's Sisters of Charity in Calcutta. Her essay on human rights and the ethnic war in Sri Lanka, "Revenge In Paradise: As We Love Our Own Lives," appears in the autumn 1993 issue of *High Plains Literary Quarterly,* and an essay on the work of PBI, "Deeper Darkness," appears in *Manoa,* summer 1995.